MEAL PREP COOKBOOK

Healthy Meal Preparation Guide for Beginners Meal Preparation is the Concept of Preparing Whole Meals or Dishes ahead of Schedule.

Table of Contents

6

Introduction

Why is this Meal Prep Cookbook release so important? Because at MEAL PREP, we believe in the power of preparing today's foods with the assurance that you'll always have healthy options to get the body and mind ready for tomorrow. This cookbook is full of easy recipes that will save you money and help you achieve your fitness goals.

In recent years, Meal Prep has become an emerging trend as people realize the benefits of spending time preparing meals in advance. Convenience, cost-effectiveness, and time-saving are the main factors contributing to the growing popularity of meal prep. If you are a busy working professional, meal prep will help you cut down on the money and time you spend on buying take-outs from the office cafeteria. It will also help you stay away from junk food and better control your caloric intake. Preparing a few portions of your favorite meals can help you save money and feel energetic enough to make it through the long and busy work schedule and daily responsibilities.

The most significant advantage of prepping your own meals is the chance to personalize your meals. This factor makes prepping meals more enjoyable and exciting. Individuals used to buy prepared meals from their local grocery stores and take their meals to work. It cost money and took up most of their time only to have it eaten in front of them while they are sitting at their desks all day.

While the benefits of meal prep can be split into two main categories: financial and health, it saves lots of your finances in the long run by reaping the benefits of cheaper food. You will also enjoy healthier eating because you already chose what and how much to eat. Not to mention, meal prep is an excellent way to stay consistent with your goals and objectives. For anyone who wants to lose weight, for example, the key to long-term success is consistency. To succeed with weight loss, you must stay in control of your diet. If you are going about it the right way and planning ahead, you will lose weight much easier than you ever thought possible.

It also allows you to eat healthy throughout the week without worrying about finding time to shop or cook. This meal prep cookbook includes a wide range of recipes so that you can use this book for multiple purposes. You can use these recipes for meal prepping, as well as making them from scratch for your family and friends.

How to Meal Prep?

There are different ways on how you can meal prep if you're a beginner in this journey. Some of them are the following:

Make-Ahead Meals

Prepare for the week ahead and freeze the meals that you plan to cook every week. This kind of meal preparation is easy and saves time in the summer. Using freezer containers is a great way to preserve food for future use. The frozen meals taste great and have fewer ingredients. You will also save your wallet on fresh groceries.

Batch Cooking

This meal prep method involves preparing multiple recipes at a time and cooking them all together. It is an excellent way to prepare several meals fast. This method's advantage is that it is economical since you can prepare large portions of food in one go.

Individually Portioned Meals

Prepare food individually and make sure they will be ready fast. This method is perfect for a week filled with celebrations. You can prepare each meal individually in the evening and enjoy the benefits of eating right out of the containers.

Ready-To-Cook Ingredients

If you're a busy person who does not have much time to cook in the morning, shopping for ready-to-cook ingredients will do. Buying and preparing fresh ingredients ahead of time will help you save time in the busy mornings. But make sure to eat fresh meals. As soon as the ingredients are bought, they will also spoil if not eaten straight away. Therefore, you need to plan your meals ahead of time to make sure you will use them before they get stale.

Now that you know the basics and advantages of meal prepping, it's time to get down to the most awaited 500 meal prep recipes with the 30-day meal plan by the end of it. We hope you'll enjoy the wide range of meals but make sure to make them in your own way. If you are a vegan, don't add meat to your recipes. If you are a vegetarian, add some meat to the recipe. Most importantly, don't fear to play around with your recipes! Happy meal prepping.

Pork Chops in Peach Glaze

Preparation Time: 15 minutes

Cooking Time: 16 minutes

Servings: 2

Ingredients:

- 2 (6-ounce) boneless pork chops, trimmed
- Sea Salt
- ground black pepper, as required
- ½ of ripe yellow peach, peeled, pitted, and chopped
- 1 tablespoon olive oil
- 2 tablespoons shallot, minced
- 2 tablespoons garlic, minced
- 2 tablespoons fresh ginger, minced
- 4-6 drops liquid stevia
- 1 tablespoon balsamic vinegar
- ¼ teaspoon red pepper flakes, crushed
- ¼ cup of filtered water

Directions:

1. Flavor the pork chops with sea salt and black pepper generously. In a blender, add the peach pieces and pulse until a puree form. Reserve the remaining peach pieces.
2. Heat-up the oil over medium heat in a skillet, and sauté the shallots for about 1-2 minutes. Put the garlic plus ginger and sauté for about 1

minute. Mix in the rest of the fixings and bring to a boil.

3. Adjust the heat to medium-low and simmer for about 4-5 minutes or until a sticky glaze form. Remove from the heat and reserve 1/3 of the glaze, and set aside.
4. Coat the chops with the remaining glaze. Heat-up a nonstick skillet over medium-high heat and sear the chops for about 4 minutes per side.
5. Transfer the chops onto a plate and coat with the remaining glaze evenly. Serve immediately.
6. Transfer the pork chops into a large bowl and set aside to cool. Divide the chops into 2 containers evenly. Cover the containers and refrigerate for 1-2 days. Reheat in the microwave before serving.

Nutrition:
Calories 359
Fat 13.5 g
Carbs 12 g
Protein 46.2 g

Ground Pork with Spinach

Preparation Time: 15 minutes
Cooking Time: 15 minutes
Servings: 4
Ingredients:

- 1 tablespoon olive oil
- ½ of white onion, chopped
- 2 garlic cloves, chopped finely
- 1 jalapeño pepper, chopped finely
- 1 pound lean ground pork
- 1 teaspoon ground coriander
- 1 teaspoon ground cumin
- ½ teaspoon ground turmeric
- ½ teaspoon ground cinnamon
- ½ teaspoon ground fennel seeds
- Salt and ground black pepper, as required
- ½ cup fresh cherry tomatoes, quartered
- 1¼ pounds collard greens leave stemmed and chopped
- 1 teaspoon fresh lemon juice

Directions:

1. Heat-up the oil over medium heat in a large skillet, and sauté the onion for about 4 minutes. Add the garlic and jalapeño pepper and sauté for about 1 minute.
2. Add the pork and spices and cook for about 6 minutes, breaking into pieces with the spoon.

Stir in the tomatoes and greens and cook, stirring gently for about 4 minutes.

3. Stir in the lemon juice and remove from heat. Serve hot.
4. Transfer the pork mixture into a large bowl and set aside to cool. Divide the mixture into 4 containers evenly. Cover the containers and refrigerate for 1-2 days. Reheat in the microwave before serving.

Nutrition:

Calories 316

Fat 21.8 g

Carbs 11.4 g

Protein 23 g

Pork Chops with Grape Sauce

Preparation Time: 15 minutes

Cooking Time: 25 minutes

Servings: 4

Ingredients:

- Cooking spray
- 4 pork chops
- ¼ cup onion, sliced
- 1 clove garlic, minced
- 1/2 cup low-sodium chicken broth
- ¾ cup apple juice
- 1 tablespoon cornstarch
- 1 tablespoon balsamic vinegar
- 1 teaspoon honey
- 1 cup red grapes, cut in half

Directions:

1. Spray oil on your pan. Put it over medium heat. Add the pork chops to the pan. Cook for 5 minutes per side. Remove and set aside.
2. Add onion and garlic—Cook for 2 minutes. Pour in the broth and apple juice; boil, then reduce heat to simmer.
3. Move the pork chops to the skillet. Simmer for 4 minutes. In a bowl, mix the cornstarch, vinegar, and honey. Add to the pan. Cook until the sauce has thickened.
4. Add the grapes. Pour sauce over the pork chops before serving.

Nutrition:
Calories 188
Fat 4 g
Carbohydrate 18 g
Protein 19 g

Roasted Pork & Apples

Preparation Time: 15 minutes

Cooking Time: 30 minutes

Servings: 4

Ingredients:

- Salt and pepper to taste
- 1/2 teaspoon dried, crushed
- 1 lb. pork tenderloin
- 1 tablespoon canola oil
- 1 onion, sliced into wedges
- 3 cooking apples, cut into wedges
- 2/3 cup apple cider
- Sprigs fresh sage

Directions:

1. In a bowl, mix salt, pepper, and sage. Season both sides of pork with this mixture. Place a pan over medium heat. Brown both sides.
2. Transfer to a roasting pan. Add the onion on top and around the pork—drizzle oil on top of the pork and apples.
3. Roast in the oven at 425 F within 10 minutes. Add the apples, roast for another 15 minutes. In a pan, boil the apple cider and then simmer for 10 minutes.
4. Pour the apple cider sauce over the pork before serving.

Nutrition:

Calories 239
Fat 6 g
Carbohydrate 22 g
Protein 24 g

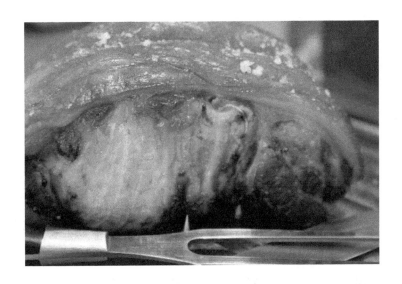

Pork with Cranberry Relish

Preparation Time: 30 minutes

Cooking Time: 30 minutes

Servings: 4

Ingredients:

- 12 oz. pork tenderloin, fat trimmed and sliced crosswise
- Salt and pepper to taste
- ¼ cup all-purpose flour
- 2 tablespoons olive oil
- 1 onion, sliced thinly
- ¼ cup dried cranberries
- ¼ cup low-sodium chicken broth
- 1 tablespoon balsamic vinegar

Directions:

1. Flatten each slice of pork using a mallet. Mix the salt, pepper, and flour in a dish. Dip each pork slice into the flour mixture.
2. Put oil in your pan on medium high heat—Cook pork for 3 minutes per side or until golden crispy.
3. Move to your serving plate and cover with foil— Cook the pan's onion for 4 minutes.
4. Stir in the rest of the ingredients. Simmer until the sauce has thickened.

Nutrition:

Calories 211

Fat 9 g
Carbohydrate 15 g
Protein 18 g

Sesame Pork with Mustard Sauce

Preparation Time: 25 minutes
Cooking Time: 25 minutes
Servings: 4
Ingredients:
- 2 tablespoons low-sodium teriyaki sauce
- ¼ cup chili sauce
- 2 cloves garlic, minced
- 2 teaspoons ginger, grated
- 2 pork tenderloins
- 2 teaspoons sesame seeds
- ¼ cup low-fat sour cream
- 1 teaspoon Dijon mustard
- Salt to taste
- 1 scallion, chopped

Directions:
1. Warm your oven to 425 degrees F. Mix the teriyaki sauce, chili sauce, garlic, and ginger. Put the pork on a roasting pan.
2. Glaze the sauce on both sides of the pork—Bake in the oven for 15 minutes. Brush with more sauce. Top with sesame seeds.
3. Roast for 10 more minutes. Mix the rest of the ingredients. Serve the pork with mustard sauce.

Nutrition:
Calories 135
Fat 3 g

Carbohydrate 7 g
Protein 20 g

Steak with Mushroom Sauce

Preparation Time: 20 minutes

Cooking Time: 5 minutes

Servings: 4

Ingredients:

- 12 oz. sirloin steak, sliced and trimmed
- 2 teaspoons grilling seasoning
- 2 teaspoons oil
- 6 oz. broccoli, trimmed
- 2 cups frozen peas
- 3 cups fresh mushrooms, sliced
- 1 cup beef broth (unsalted)
- 1 tablespoon mustard
- 2 teaspoons cornstarch
- Salt to taste

Directions:

1. Warm your oven to 350 degrees F. Season meat with grilling seasoning. In a pan over medium-high heat, cook the meat and broccoli for 4 minutes.
2. Sprinkle the peas around the steak. Put the pan inside your oven and bake within 8 minutes. Remove both meat and vegetables from the pan.
3. Add the mushrooms to the pan—Cook for 3 minutes. Mix the broth, mustard, salt, and cornstarch; add to the mushrooms—Cook for 1

minute. Pour sauce over meat and vegetables before serving.

Nutrition:

Calories 226

Fat 6

Carbohydrate 16 g

Protein 26 g

Steak with Tomato & Herbs

Preparation Time: 30 minutes

Cooking Time: 30 minutes

Servings: 2

Ingredients:

- 8 oz. beef loin steak, sliced in half
- Salt and pepper to taste
- Cooking spray
- 1 teaspoon fresh basil, snipped
- ¼ cup green onion, sliced
- 1/2 cup tomato, chopped

Directions:

1. Season the steak with salt and pepper. Spray oil on your pan. Put the pan over medium-high heat. Once hot, add the steaks.
2. Reduce heat to medium. Cook for 10 to 13 minutes for medium, turning once. Add the basil and green onion—Cook for 2 minutes. Add the tomato—Cook for 1 minute. Let cool a little before slicing.

Nutrition:

Calories 170

Fat 6 g

Carbohydrate 3 g

Protein 25 g

Barbecue Beef Brisket

Preparation Time: 25 minutes
Cooking Time: 10 hours
Servings: 10
Ingredients:

- 4 lb. beef brisket (boneless), trimmed and sliced
- 1 bay leaf
- 2 onions, sliced into rings
- 1/2 teaspoon dried thyme, crushed
- ¼ cup chili sauce
- 1 clove garlic, minced
- Salt and pepper to taste
- 2 tablespoons light brown sugar
- 2 tablespoons cornstarch
- 2 tablespoons cold water

Directions:

1. Put the meat in a slow cooker. Add the bay leaf and onion. In a bowl, mix the thyme, chili sauce, salt, pepper, and sugar. Pour the sauce over the meat. Mix well.
2. Seal the pot and cook on low heat for 10 hours. Discard the bay leaf. Pour cooking liquid in a pan; put the mixed water and cornstarch. Simmer until the sauce has thickened. Pour the sauce over the meat.

Nutrition:
Calories 182

Fat 6 g
Protein 20 g

Beef & Asparagus

Preparation Time: 15 minutes
Cooking Time: 10 minutes
Servings: 4
Ingredients:
- 2 teaspoons olive oil
- 1 lb. lean beef sirloin, trimmed and sliced
- 1 carrot, shredded
- Salt and pepper to taste
- 12 oz. asparagus, trimmed and sliced
- 1 teaspoon dried herbs de Provence, crushed
- 1/2 cup Marsala
- ¼ teaspoon lemon zest

Directions:
1. Put oil in your pan on medium heat. Put the beef and carrot. Season with salt and pepper. Cook for 3 minutes. Add the asparagus and herbs.
2. Cook for 2 minutes. Add the Marsala and lemon zest. Cook for 5 minutes, stirring frequently. Serve, or store until ready to eat.

Nutrition:
Calories 327
Fat 7 g
Carbohydrate 29 g
Protein 28 g

Italian Beef

Preparation Time: 20 minutes
Cooking Time: 1 hour and 20 minutes
Servings: 4
Ingredients:

- Cooking spray
- 1 lb. beef round steak, trimmed and sliced
- 1 cup onion, chopped
- 2 cloves garlic, minced
- 1 cup green bell pepper, chopped
- 1/2 cup celery, chopped
- 2 cups mushrooms, sliced
- 14 1/2 oz. canned diced tomatoes
- 1/2 teaspoon dried basil
- ¼ teaspoon dried oregano
- 1/8 teaspoon crushed red pepper
- 2 tablespoons Parmesan cheese, grated

Directions:

1. Spray oil on the pan over medium heat. Cook the meat until brown on both sides. Transfer meat to a plate. Add the onion, garlic, bell pepper, celery, and mushroom to the pan.
2. Cook until tender. Add the tomatoes, herbs, and pepper. Put the meat back in the pan. Simmer while covered for 1 hour and 15 minutes.
3. Stir occasionally. Sprinkle Parmesan cheese on top of the dish before serving.

Nutrition:
Calories 212
Fat 4 g
Carbs 1 g
Protein 30 g

Lamb with Broccoli & Carrots

Preparation Time: 20 minutes
Cooking Time: 10 minutes
Servings: 4
Ingredients:

- 2 cloves garlic, minced
- 1 tablespoon fresh ginger, grated
- ¼ teaspoon red pepper, crushed
- 2 tablespoons low-sodium soy sauce
- 1 tablespoon white vinegar
- 1 tablespoon cornstarch
- 12 oz. lamb meat, trimmed and sliced
- 2 teaspoons cooking oil
- 1 lb. broccoli, cut into florets
- 2 carrots, cut into strips
- ¾ cup low-sodium beef broth
- 4 green onions, chopped
- 2 cups cooked spaghetti squash pasta

Directions:

1. Combine the garlic, ginger, red pepper, soy sauce, vinegar, and cornstarch in a bowl. Add lamb to the marinade. Marinate for 10 minutes. Discard marinade.
2. Put the oil in a pan on medium heat. Put the lamb and cook for 3 minutes—Transfer lamb to a plate. Add the broccoli and carrots.

3. Cook for 1 minute. Pour in the beef broth—Cook for 5 minutes. Put the meat back in the pan. Sprinkle with green onion and serve on top of spaghetti squash.

Nutrition:
Calories 205
Fat 6 g
Protein 1 g
Carbohydrate 17 g

Rosemary Lamb

Preparation Time: 15 minutes
Cooking Time: 2 hours
Servings: 14
Ingredients:
- Salt and pepper to taste
- 2 teaspoons fresh rosemary, snipped
- 5 lb. the whole leg of lamb, trimmed and cut with slits on all sides
- 3 cloves garlic, slivered
- 1 cup of water

Directions:
1. Warm your oven to 375 degrees F. Mix salt, pepper, and rosemary in a bowl. Sprinkle mixture all over the lamb. Insert slivers of garlic into the slits.
2. Put the lamb on a roasting pan. Add water to the pan—roast for 2 hours. Serve or store until ready to eat.

Nutrition:
Calories 136
Fat 4 g
Carbs 1 g
Protein 23 g

Mediterranean Lamb Meatballs

Preparation Time: 10 minutes

Cooking Time: 20 minutes

Servings: 8

Ingredients:

- 12 oz. roasted red peppers
- 1 1/2 cups whole wheat breadcrumbs
- 2 eggs, beaten
- 1/3 cup tomato sauce
- 1/2 cup fresh basil
- ¼ cup parsley snipped
- Salt and pepper to taste
- 2 lb. lean ground lamb

Directions:

1. Warm your oven to 350 degrees F. In a bowl, mix all the ingredients and form them into meatballs. Put the meatballs on a baking pan. Bake in the oven for 20 minutes.

Nutrition:

Calories 94

Fat 3 g

Protein 1 g

Carbohydrate 2 g

Vegetables

Portobello Mushroom Pizza

Preparation Time: 15 minutes

Cooking Time: 5 minutes

Servings: 4

Ingredients:

- 4 large portobello mushrooms, stems removed
- ¼ cup olive oil
- 1 teaspoon minced garlic
- 1 medium tomato, cut into 4 slices
- 2 teaspoons chopped fresh basil
- 1 cup shredded mozzarella cheese

Directions:

1. Preheat the oven to broil. Prepare your baking sheet with aluminum foil, then set aside. In a small bowl, toss the mushroom caps with the olive oil until well coated.
2. Rub the oil in using your fingertips without breaking the mushrooms. Put the mushrooms on the baking sheet gill-side down and broil the mushrooms until they are tender on the tops, about 2 minutes
3. Flip the mushrooms over and broil 1 minute more. Take the baking sheet out and spread the garlic over each mushroom, top each with a tomato slice, sprinkle with the basil, and top with the cheese
4. Broil the mushrooms until the cheese is melted and bubbly, about 1 minute. Serve.

Nutrition:
Calories: 251
Fat: 20g
Protein: 14g
Carbs: 7g

Garlicky Green Beans

Preparation Time: 10 minutes
Cooking Time: 10 minutes
Servings: 4
Ingredients:

- 1 pound green beans, stemmed
- 2 tablespoons olive oil
- 1 teaspoon minced garlic
- Sea salt
- Freshly ground black pepper
- ¼ cup freshly grated Parmesan cheese

Directions:

1. Preheat the oven to 425°F. Prepare your baking sheet with aluminum foil, then set aside. In a large bowl, toss together the green beans, olive oil, and garlic until well mixed. Flavor the beans lightly with salt plus pepper.
2. Put the beans on your baking sheet, then roast them until they are tender and lightly browned, stirring them once, about 10 minutes. Serve topped with the Parmesan cheese.

Nutrition:
Calories: 104
Fat: 9g
Protein: 4g
Carbs: 2g

Sautéed Asparagus with Walnuts

Preparation Time: 10 minutes

Cooking Time: 5 minutes

Servings: 4

Ingredients:
- 1½ tablespoons olive oil
- ¾ pound asparagus, woody ends trimmed
- Sea salt
- Freshly ground pepper
- ¼ cup chopped walnuts

Directions:
1. Put your large skillet on medium-high heat and add the olive oil. Sauté the asparagus until the spears are tender and lightly browned, about 5 minutes.
2. Season the asparagus with salt and pepper. Remove the skillet and toss the asparagus with the walnuts. Serve.

Nutrition:

Calories: 124

Fat: 12g

Protein: 3g

Carbs: 4g

Creamed Spinach

Preparation Time: 10 minutes
Cooking Time: 30 minutes
Servings: 4
Ingredients:

- 1 tablespoon butter
- ½ sweet onion, very thinly sliced
- 4 cups spinach, stemmed and thoroughly washed
- ¾ cup heavy (whipping) cream
- ¼ cup Herbed Chicken Stock
- Pinch sea salt
- Pinch freshly ground black pepper
- Pinch ground nutmeg

Directions:

1. Put the butter in your large skillet over medium heat. Sauté the onion until it is lightly caramelized, about 5 minutes.
2. Stir in the spinach, heavy cream, chicken stock, salt, pepper, and nutmeg. Sauté until the spinach is wilted, about 5 minutes.
3. Continue cooking the spinach until it is tender and the sauce is thickened about 15 minutes. Serve or store.

Nutrition:
Calories: 195
Fat: 20g

Protein: 3g
Carbs: 3g

Cheesy Mashed Cauliflower

Preparation Time: 15 minutes

Cooking Time: 5 minutes

Servings: 4

Ingredients:

- 1 head cauliflower, chopped roughly
- ½ cup shredded Cheddar cheese
- ¼ cup heavy (whipping) cream
- 2 tablespoons butter, at room temperature
- Sea salt
- Freshly ground black pepper

Directions:

1. Put a large saucepan filled 3-quarters full with water over high heat and boil. Blanch the cauliflower until tender, within 5 minutes, and drain.
2. Move the cauliflower to your food processor and add the cheese, heavy cream, and butter. Purée until very creamy and whipped—season with salt and pepper. Serve.

Nutrition:

Calories: 183

Fat: 15g

Protein: 8g

Carbs: 6g

Sautéed Crispy Zucchini

Preparation Time: 15 minutes
Cooking Time: 10 minutes
Servings: 4
Ingredients:

- 2 tablespoons butter
- 4 zucchinis, cut into ¼-inch-thick rounds
- ½ cup freshly grated Parmesan cheese
- Freshly ground black pepper

Directions:

1. Place a large skillet on medium-high heat, then melt the butter. Put the zucchini, then sauté until tender and lightly browned, about 5 minutes.
2. Put the zucchini in the skillet and sprinkle the Parmesan cheese over the vegetables. Cook without stirring until the Parmesan cheese is melted and crispy where it touches the skillet, about 5 minutes. Serve.

Nutrition:
Calories: 94
Fat: 8g
Protein: 4g
Carbs: 1g

Mushrooms with Camembert

Preparation Time: 5 minutes

Cooking Time: 15 minutes

Servings: 4

Ingredients:
- 2 tablespoons butter
- 2 teaspoons minced garlic
- 1 pound button mushrooms, halved
- 4 ounces Camembert cheese, diced
- Freshly ground black pepper

Directions:
1. Put your skillet on medium-high heat and melt the butter. Sauté the garlic until translucent, about 3 minutes.
2. Sauté the mushrooms until tender, about 10 minutes. Stir in the cheese and sauté until melted, about 2 minutes; season with pepper and serve.

Nutrition:

Calories: 161

Fat: 13g

Protein: 9g

Carbs: 4g

Pesto Zucchini Noodles

Preparation Time: 15 minutes

Cooking Time: 10 minutes

Servings: 4

Ingredients:

- 4 small zucchinis, ends trimmed
- ¾ cup Herb Kale Pesto, ¼ cup grated or shredded
- Parmesan cheese

Directions:

1. Slice the zucchini into noodles using your spiralizer or peeler and place them in a medium bowl. Add the pesto and the Parmesan cheese and toss to coat. Serve.

Nutrition:

Calories: 93

Fat: 8g

Protein: 4g

Carbs: 2g

Golden Rosti

Preparation Time: 15 minutes
Cooking Time: 15 minutes
Servings: 8
Ingredients:

- 8 bacon slices, chopped
- 1 cup shredded acorn squash
- 1 cup shredded raw celeriac
- 2 tablespoons grated or shredded Parmesan cheese
- 2 teaspoons minced garlic
- 1 teaspoon chopped fresh thyme
- Sea salt
- Freshly ground black pepper
- 2 tablespoons butter

Directions:

1. Cook the bacon in your large skillet on medium-high heat, about 5 minutes.
2. While the bacon is cooking, mix the squash, celeriac, Parmesan cheese, garlic, and thyme in a large bowl. Flavor the mixture generously with salt and pepper, and set aside.
3. Remove the cooked bacon with a slotted spoon to the rosti mixture and stir to incorporate. Remove all but leave 2 tbsp of bacon fat from the skillet and put the butter

4. Adjust the heat to medium-low and move the rosti batter to the skillet, and put it out to form a large round patty about 1 inch thick.
5. Cook within 5 minutes; flip the rosti over and cook until the other side is crispy and the middle is cooked through, about 5 minutes more.
6. Remove the skillet from the heat and cut the rosti into 8 pieces. Serve.

Nutrition:

Calories: 171

Fat: 15g

Protein: 5g

Carbs: 3g

Artichoke and Avocado Pasta Salad

Preparation Time: 15 minutes
Cooking Time: 30 minutes
Servings: 10 servings
Ingredients:

- 2 cups of spiral pasta (uncooked)
- A quarter cup of Romano cheese (grated)
- 1 can of artichoke hearts (coarsely chopped and drained well)
- 1 avocado (medium-sized, ripe, cubed)
- 2 plum tomatoes (chopped coarsely)

For the dressing:

- 1 tbsp. of fresh cilantro (chopped)
- 2 tbsps. of lime juice
- A quarter cup of canola oil
- 1 and a half tsp of lime zest (grated)

1/2 tsp each of:

- Pepper (freshly ground)
- Kosher salt

Directions:

1. Follow the directions mentioned on the package for cooking the pasta. Drain them well and rinse using cold water.
2. Then, take a large-sized bowl and add the pasta along with the tomatoes, artichoke hearts, cheese, and avocado. Combine them well.

3. Then, take another bowl and add all the ingredients of the dressing to it. Whisk them together and, once combined, add the dressing over the pasta.
4. Gently toss the mixture to coat everything evenly in the dressing and then refrigerate.

Nutrition:

Calories: 188

Protein: 6g

Fat: 10g

Carbs: 21g

Apple Arugula and Turkey Salad in a Jar

Preparation Time: 10 minutes
Cooking Time: 10 minutes
Servings: 4
Ingredients:

- 3 tbsps. of red wine vinegar
- 2 tbsps. of chives (freshly minced)
- 1/2 cup of orange juice
- 1-3 tbsps. of sesame oil
- A quarter tsp. each of:
- Pepper (coarsely ground)
- Salt

For the salad:

- 4 tsp of curry powder
- 4 cups each of
- Turkey (cubed, cooked)
- Baby spinach or fresh arugula
- A quarter tsp. of salt
- 1/2 tsp. of pepper (coarsely ground)
- 1 cup of halved green grapes
- 1 apple (large-sized, chopped)
- 11 oz. of mandarin oranges (properly drained)
- 1 tbsp. of lemon juice

1/2 a cup each of:

- Walnuts (chopped)

- Dried cranberries or pomegranate seeds

Directions:

1. Take a small-sized bowl and, in it, add the first 6 ingredients from the list. Whisk them. Then take a large bowl and add the turkey, and then add the seasonings on top of it.
2. Toss the turkey cubes to coat them with the seasoning. Take another bowl and add the lemon juice and toss the apple chunks in the juice.
3. Take four jars and divide the layers in order. First goes the orange juice mixture. The second layer is the turkey, then apple, oranges, grapes, cranberries or pomegranate seeds, walnuts, spinach, or arugula. Cover the jars and then refrigerate them.

Nutrition:

Calories: 471

Protein: 45g

Fat: 19g

Carbs: 33g

Summertime Slaw

Preparation Time: 20 minutes
Cooking Time: 30 minutes
Servings: 10-12
Ingredients:

- 1/3 cup of canola oil
- 3/4 cups each of:
- White vinegar
- Sugar

1 tsp. each of:

- Pepper
- Salt
- 1 tbsp. of water
- 1/2 tsp red pepper flakes, crushed)
- 2 tomatoes (medium-sized, seeded, peeled, and chopped)
- 1 pack of coleslaw mix (fourteen oz.)
- 1 sweet red pepper (small-sized, chopped)
- 1 green pepper (small-sized, chopped)
- 1 onion (large-sized, chopped)
- 1/2 cup of sweet pickle relish

Directions:

1. Take a saucepan of large size and in it, combine water, sugar, oil, vinegar, pepper, salt, and if you want, then red pepper flakes too.
2. Cook them over medium heat by continuously stirring the mixture. Keep mixing until it boils.

Cook within another two minutes or so and make sure that all the sugar has dissolved.

3. Once done, cool the mixture to room temperature by stirring it. Take a salad bowl of large size, and in it, combine the pickle relish, coleslaw mix, peppers, onion, and tomatoes.

4. On top of the mixture, add the dressing and toss the mixture to coat it properly. Cover the mixture and put it in the refrigerator for a night.

Nutrition:

Calories: 138

Protein: 1g

Fat: 6g

Carbs: 21g

Zucchini and Tomato Spaghetti

Preparation Time: 10 minutes

Cooking Time: 20 minutes

Servings: 4 servings

Ingredients:

- 2 large-sized zucchinis nicely spiralized
- 3 cups of red and yellow cherry tomatoes
- 4 oz. of spaghetti (whole wheat – optional)
- Toppings – grated parmesan

For the avocado sauce:

- 3/4 cup of olive oil
- 1 avocado
- 1/2 cup of parsley (fresh)
- 1/2 tsp. of salt
- 3/4 green onions (only the green parts)
- 1 lemon (juiced)
- 1 clove of garlic
- A pinch of pepper (freshly ground)

Directions:

1. Firstly, take all the sauce ingredients and pulse them so that they are combined well and form a smooth mixture. Set it aside.
2. Then, follow the directions mentioned in the package for cooking the spaghetti. Drain the cooked spaghetti and keep it aside too.
3. Take a large-sized skillet and heat the cherry tomatoes in it. Use a bit of olive oil. Keep

cooking the tomatoes until they seem well-roasted, and they will also seem loosened with their skins split. Once done, remove the tomatoes from the flame and set them aside.

4. Then, add the zucchini to the same skillet. Stir and toss them for about two minutes until they look crisp. Then, add the avocado sauce and the spaghetti.

5. Keep tossing until everything has properly combined. Flavor with pepper and salt as per taste. Top with parmesan and the tomatoes that you had reserved earlier.

Nutrition:

Calories: 330

Protein: 7.1g

Fat: 20g

Carbs: 35.3g

White Bean Salad

Preparation Time: 5 minutes

Cooking Time: 10 minutes

Servings: 4 servings

Ingredients:

For the salad:

- 2 green peppers coarsely chopped
- 1/2 cup each of
- Chopped cucumber
- Chopped tomatoes
- 1 1/2 cups of white beans (boiled)
- 3/4 cup each of
- Green onions (chopped)
- Fresh dill (chopped)
- Parsley (chopped)
- 4 eggs (hard-boiled)

For the dressing:

- 1 tbsp. of lemon juice
- 1 tsp. of vinegar
- 2 tbsps. of olive oil
- 1 tsp. of sumac
- 1/2 tsp. of salt

For quick onion pickle:

1 tsp. each of:

- Sumac
- Salt
- Vinegar

- 1 tbsp. of lemon juice
- 2 thinly sliced red onions (medium-sized)
- 2 cups of water (hot)

Directions:
1. Take a large-sized bowl and add all the salad ingredients in it, but keep the eggs aside.
2. In case you do not want to pickle the onions, you can simply make thin slices and then mix them with the other fixings.
3. Take all the ingredients of the dressing together in one bowl and whisk them together. Then, drizzle the dressing over the salad. Toss well, and on the top, place halved eggs.
4. For the pickled onions, take very hot water and place the sliced onions in it. Blanch the onions within one minute and then immediately transfer them into a pot of very cold water so that the cooking stops.
5. Let them stay in that pot of cold water for a few minutes. Once done, drain them well.
6. Mix sumac, lemon juice, salt, and vinegar, and then pour the mixture over the onion that you just drained. Keep it for 5 to 10 minutes.
7. Then, add the onions into the mixture of salad and stir well. Keep some onions aside so that you can use them as a topping.

Nutrition:

Calories: 449
Protein: 23.6g
Fat: 23.3g
Carbs: 39.7g

Lentil Bolognese

Preparation Time: 20 minutes
Cooking Time: 40 minutes
Servings: 4-6 servings
Ingredients:

- 2 boxes of penne pasta
- 1 onion (medium-sized, finely chopped)
- 1 red bell pepper (finely chopped)
- 2 tbsps. of olive oil
- 2 carrots (large-sized, sliced)
- 4 cloves of garlic (large ones, minced)
- 1 tbsp. of miso

1 tsp. each of:

- Pepper
- Salt
- 4 cups of water
- 1 can of tomato paste (measuring five and a half ounces)

1 cup each of

- Brown lentils (dried)
- Cherry tomatoes (halved)
- Toppings (optional) – black pepper, sage leaves, parmesan (grated)

Directions:

1. Take a large-sized skillet and start by heating the oil in it on medium flame. Then, add the chopped onions.
2. In about five minutes, they will soften and appear to be translucent. Then, add the red pepper, carrots, sugar, and sea salt to the skillet and keep cooking.
3. Stir the mixture from time to time. In fifteen minutes, everything will be well caramelized. Then, add the tomato paste and the garlic and let the mixture cook for three minutes or until you get a caramelized fragrance from the paste.
4. Then, add the lentils, miso, and water to the skillet and bring the mixture to a boil. Once the batter is boiling, reduce the flame and keep the skillet uncovered while the lentils are cooking. It will take about twenty-five to thirty minutes.
5. Keep stirring the lentils from time to time, and in case they look dry, add some water. After that, add the cherry tomatoes and keep stirring.
6. While you are cooking the lentils, take a large pot and fill it with water. Add generous amounts of salt and bring the water to a boil.
7. Then, add the chickpea pasta into the water and cook it for about five to six minutes or until al dente. Don't overcook it. Strain the water, then set them aside to cool.

8. Divide the penne into four to six meal prep containers and top with Bolognese. Sprinkle a few sage leaves or a bit of parmesan if you want.

Nutrition:
Calories: 486
Protein: 29.3g
Fat: 9g
Carbs: 78.2g

Kale, Lemon, and White Bean Soup

Preparation Time: 20 minutes
Cooking Time: 1 hour 10 minutes
Servings: 2
Ingredients:

- 150 grams of dried cannellini beans
- 2 cups of vegetable stock
- 5 cups of water
- 1 white onion (large-sized, diced)
- 2 tbsps. of olive oil
- 8 cloves of garlic
- Kombu (one-inch strip)
- 1 tsp. of dried thyme
- 2 potatoes (small ones, cubed after peeling)
- 2 bay leaves
- 1 cup of kale
- 1 lemon (juiced and zest)

Directions:

1. Take ample water to soak the dried beans and keep them soaked for about twelve hours. Drain the beans properly, and they should become double their size. Rinse them, and they are ready to be cooked.
2. Take a large-sized pot, and in it, add one tbsp of oil and heat it. Put the diced onion to the pot and cook the onions until they become golden and soft.

3. Then, add the stock and water and garlic, dried beans, kombu, thyme, and bay leaves. Keep the pot covered, and then bring it to a boil. Once it starts boiling, adjust the flame to a simmer and wait for about forty minutes.
4. While it is cooking, start with the kale. Wash it thoroughly. All the tough inner stalks should be removed.
5. Then, start slicing them into ribbons of one-inch each. It looks good when you have delicate small pieces, so you should take your time with this.
6. After 1/2 hour, put the potatoes in the pot and then let the preparation simmer for ten more minutes. After this, both the potatoes and the beans should be soft.
7. Take out the kombu and bay leaves. Take a potato masher and use it carefully to mash at least half of the beans and potatoes.
8. Add the kale—Cook the mixture for ten more minutes. The water content needs to be checked now and see whether it is right or whether it needs to be topped up a bit.
9. Once you notice the kale softening, take a tbsp of olive oil and add it to the pot. Stir in the zest and lemon juice as well, and your dish is ready.

Nutrition:
Calories: 574

Protein: 22g
Fat: 16g
Carbs: 106g

Aloo Gobi

Preparation Time: 15 Minutes
Cooking Time: 4 To 5 Hours
Servings: 4
Ingredients:
- 1 large cauliflower, cut into 1-inch pieces
- 1 large russet potato, peeled and diced
- 1 medium yellow onion, peeled and diced
- 1 cup canned diced tomatoes, with juice
- 1 cup frozen peas
- ¼ cup of water
- 1 (2-inch) piece ginger, peeled & finely chopped
- 1½ teaspoons minced garlic (3 cloves)
- 1 jalapeño pepper, stemmed and sliced
- 1 tablespoon cumin seeds
- 1 tablespoon garam masala
- 1 teaspoon ground turmeric
- 1 heaping tablespoon fresh cilantro
- Cooked rice, for serving (optional)

Directions:
1. Combine the cauliflower, potato, onion, diced tomatoes, peas, water, ginger, garlic, jalapeño, cumin seeds, garam masala, and turmeric in a slow cooker; mix until well combined.
2. Cover and cook on low within 4 to 5 hours. Garnish with cilantro, and serve over cooked rice (if using).

Nutrition:
Calories: 115
Fat: 1g
Protein: 6g
Carbs: 0g

Jackfruit Carnitas

Preparation Time: 15 Minutes

Cooking Time: 8 Hours

Servings: 4

Ingredients:
- 2 (20-ounce) cans jackfruit, drained, hard pieces discarded
- ¾ cup Vegetable Broth
- 1 tablespoon ground cumin
- 1 tablespoon dried oregano
- 1½ teaspoons ground coriander
- 1 teaspoon minced garlic (2 cloves)
- ½ teaspoon ground cinnamon
- 2 bay leaves
- Tortillas, for serving
- Optional toppings: diced onions, sliced radishes, fresh cilantro, lime wedges, Nacho Cheese

Directions:
1. Combine the jackfruit, vegetable broth, cumin, oregano, coriander, garlic, cinnamon, and bay leaves in a slow cooker. Stir to combine.
2. Cover and cook on low within 8 hours or on high for 4 hours. Use two forks to pull the jackfruit anto shreds. Remove the bay leaves. Serve with warmed tortillas plus your favorite taco fixings.

Nutrition:

Calories: 286

Fat: 2g
Protein: 6g
Carbs: 0g

Baked Beans

Preparation Time: 15 Minutes
Cooking Time: 6 Hours
Servings: 4
Ingredients:

- 2 cans white beans, drained & rinsed
- 1 (15-ounce) can tomato sauce
- 1 medium yellow onion, finely diced
- 1½ teaspoons minced garlic (3 cloves)
- 3 tablespoons brown sugar
- 2 tablespoons molasses
- 1 tablespoon prepared yellow mustard
- 1 tablespoon chili powder
- 1 teaspoon soy sauce
- Pinch salt
- Freshly ground black pepper

Directions:
1. Place the beans, tomato sauce, onion, garlic, brown sugar, molasses, mustard, chili powder, and soy sauce into a slow cooker; mix well. Cover and cook on low within 6 hours. Season with salt and pepper before serving.

Nutrition:
Calories: 468
Fat: 2g
Protein: 28g
Carbs: 0g

Brussels Sprouts Curry

Preparation Time: 15 Minutes
Cooking Time: 7 To 8 Hours
Servings: 4
Ingredients:

- ¾ pound Brussels sprouts, bottoms cut off and sliced in half
- 1 can full-fat coconut milk
- 1 cup Vegetable Broth
- 1 medium onion, diced
- 1 medium carrot, thinly sliced
- 1 medium red or Yukon potato, diced
- 1½ teaspoons minced garlic (3 cloves)
- 1 piece ginger, peeled and minced
- 1 small serrano chili, chopped
- 2 tablespoons peanut butter
- 1 tablespoon rice vinegar or other vinegar
- 1 tablespoon cane sugar or agave nectar
- 1 tablespoon soy sauce
- 1 teaspoon curry powder
- 1 teaspoon ground turmeric
- Pinch salt
- Freshly ground black pepper
- Cooked rice, for serving (optional)

Directions:

1. Place the Brussels sprouts, coconut milk, vegetable broth, onion, carrot, potato, garlic,

---

ginger, serrano chili, peanut butter, vinegar, cane sugar, soy sauce, curry powder, and turmeric in a slow cooker. Mix well.
2. Cover and cook on low within 7 to 8 hours or on high for 4 to 5 hours—season with salt and pepper. Serve over rice (if using).

Nutrition:
Calories: 404
Fat: 29g
Protein: 10g
Carbs: 8g

Coconut Green Beans

Preparation time: 15 minutes

Cooking time: 15 minutes

Servings: 6

Ingredients:

- 1 pound green beans, trimmed
- 2 tablespoons coconut oil
- Sea salt
- Freshly ground black pepper
- Shredded unsweetened coconut, for garnish (optional)

Directions:

1. Boil a large pot with water on high heat. Add the green beans. Boil the beans for 12 to 14 minutes, or until they reach your desired tenderness. Strain and return the beans to the pot.
2. Add the coconut oil and stir to coat the beans. The oil will melt quickly due to the temperature of the green beans.
3. Season with salt and pepper. Top with the coconut (if using). Refrigerate the beans in an airtight container for up to 5 days.

Nutrition:

Calories: 63

Fat: 5g

Protein: 1g

Carbs: 5g

Roasted Herb Carrots

Preparation time: 15 minutes
Cooking time: 25 minutes
Servings: 4
Ingredients:

- 2½ pounds carrots, quartered
- 2 tablespoons olive oil or avocado oil
- ¼ cup Clean Ranch Seasoning, or low-sodium ranch dressing mix
- Salt
- Freshly ground black pepper

Directions:

1. Preheat the oven to 425°F. Line a baking sheet with aluminum foil.
2. On your prepared baking sheet, mix the carrots with the olive oil. Sprinkle with the ranch seasoning and season with salt and pepper. Shake the pan, so the carrots are in a single layer.
3. Roast for 25 minutes, or until browned and bubbly. Let cool and portion the carrots into 4 single-serving 24-ounce meal prep containers. Refrigerate for up to 5 days.

Nutrition:
Calories: 191
Fat: 7g
Protein: 2g
Carbs: 31g

Cauliflower Fried Rice

Preparation time: 15 minutes

Cooking time: 11 minutes

Servings: 1

Ingredients:
- ½ shallot, minced
- ½ garlic clove, minced
- 2 cups frozen riced cauliflower
- 1/3 cup frozen peas, thawed
- 1/3 cup frozen corn, thawed
- ½ cup liquid egg whites
- 1½ teaspoons sesame oil or olive oil
- 1½ teaspoons soy sauce

Directions:
1. In a sauté pan or skillet over medium-high heat, sauté the shallot and garlic for 2 to 3 minutes, stirring, or until tender.
2. Add the cauliflower rice and cook for 3 to 4 minutes more, frequently stirring, until warm.
3. Add the peas, corn, and egg whites to the cauliflower rice and cook, stirring, for 3 to 4 minutes, until the eggs look scrambled.
4. Stir in the sesame oil and soy sauce. Let cool before transferring to a single-serving 24-ounce meal prep container. Refrigerate for up to 4 days.

Nutrition:

Calories: 273
Fat: 8g
Protein: 22g
Carbs: 30g

Sheet Pan Rainbow Veggies

Preparation time: 15 minutes

Cooking time: 15 minutes

Servings: 6

Ingredients:

- Nonstick cooking spray
- 2 cups broccoli florets, cut into large dice
- 2 cups whole button mushrooms
- 2 cups butternut squash, chopped small
- 1 zucchini, chopped small
- 1 yellow squash, chopped small
- 1 red bell pepper, chopped small
- 1 onion, chopped into 1-inch pieces
- 2 tablespoons olive oil
- 2 tablespoons balsamic vinegar
- 4 garlic cloves, minced
- 2 tablespoons dried thyme
- Salt
- Freshly ground black pepper

Directions:

1. Preheat the oven to 425°F. Prepare a sheet pan lined with your aluminum foil and coat it with cooking spray.
2. On the prepared sheet pan, toss together the broccoli, mushrooms, butternut squash, zucchini, yellow squash, red bell pepper, onion, olive oil, vinegar, garlic, and thyme. Season it

with salt and pepper. Arrange the vegetables in a single layer.

3. Roast within 12 to 15 minutes, or until tender and slightly browned. Let cool before evenly dividing the vegetables among 6 single-serving 24-ounce meal prep containers. Refrigerate for up to 3 days.

Nutrition:
Calories: 107
Fat: 5g
Protein: 4g
Carbs: 15g

Garlic-Lemon Roasted Broccoli

Preparation time: 15 minutes

Cooking time: 15 minutes

Servings: 4

Ingredients:

- Nonstick cooking spray
- 4 cups fresh broccoli florets
- 2 to 3 tablespoons olive oil
- 2 garlic cloves, minced
- Juice of 1 lemon
- ½ cup grated Parmesan cheese, divided
- Salt
- Freshly ground black pepper

Directions:

1. Preheat the oven to 425°F. Prepare a sheet pan lined with your aluminum foil and coat it with cooking spray.
2. On the prepared sheet pan, toss together the broccoli, olive oil, garlic, lemon juice, and ¼ cup of Parmesan cheese. Season with salt and pepper. Put the broccoli into a single layer on the sheet pan.
3. Bake for 12 to 15 minutes, or until tender, checking every 5 minutes to shake the pan, so it cooks evenly. Remove and sprinkle the broccoli with the remaining ¼ cup of Parmesan cheese.

4. Let cool before dividing the broccoli among 4 single-serving 24-ounce meal prep containers. Refrigerate for up to 3 days.

Nutrition:
Calories: 141
Fat: 10g
Protein: 7g
Carbs: 7g

Savory Sweet Potatoes

Preparation time: 15 minutes

Cooking time: 35 minutes

Servings: 4

Ingredients:

- Nonstick cooking spray
- 2 large sweet potatoes, slice into bite-size pieces
- 1 tablespoon olive oil
- 1 teaspoon paprika
- 1 teaspoon dried thyme
- ½ teaspoon dried parsley
- ¼ teaspoon salt

Directions:

1. Preheat the oven to 450°F. Line a sheet pan with your aluminum foil and coat it with cooking spray.
2. On the prepared sheet pan, toss together the sweet potatoes and olive oil to coat. Add the paprika, thyme, parsley, and salt and toss again to combine. Put the sweet potatoes into a single layer.
3. Bake for 30 to 35 minutes, or until the sweet potatoes are tender. Let cool before dividing among 4 single-serving 24-ounce meal prep containers. Refrigerate for up to 4 days.

Nutrition:

Calories: 89
Fat: 4g
Protein: 1g
Carbs: 14g

Oven-Roasted Asparagus

Preparation time: 15 minutes

Cooking time: 8 minutes

Servings: 4

Ingredients:

- Nonstick cooking spray
- 8 ounces asparagus, rinsed, woody ends trimmed by 1 inch, dried
- ½ teaspoon salt
- ½ teaspoon freshly ground black pepper
- 3 garlic cloves, minced
- 3 tablespoons grated Parmesan cheese

Directions:

1. Preheat the oven to 425°F. Line a sheet pan with your aluminum foil and coat it with cooking spray. Spread the asparagus into a single layer on the prepared sheet pan.
2. In a small bowl, stir the salt, pepper, garlic, and Parmesan cheese. Lightly coat the asparagus with cooking spray. Sprinkle with the Parmesan mixture.
3. Using your hands, mix the asparagus with all the ingredients and spread them into an even layer again. Lightly coat once more with cooking spray.
4. Bake for 8 minutes. Let cool before dividing the asparagus among 4 single-serving 24-ounce

meal prep containers. Refrigerate for up to 3 days.

Nutrition:
Calories: 39
Fat: 2g
Protein: 4g
Carbs: 3g

Cucumber and Tomato Salad

Preparation time: 15 minutes

Cooking time: 0 minutes

Servings: 4

Ingredients:

- 3 Roma tomatoes, seeded and diced
- 1 English cucumber, seeded and diced
- 1 red bell pepper, slice into small dice
- ½ red onion, finely diced
- ½ cup fresh parsley, chopped
- Juice of ½ lemon
- 3 tablespoons olive oil
- Salt
- Freshly ground black pepper

Directions:

1. Combine the tomatoes, cucumber, red bell pepper, red onion, and parsley in a medium bowl. Put the lemon juice plus olive oil and season with salt and pepper. Gently mix until combined.
2. Evenly divide the salad among 4 single-serving 24-ounce meal prep containers. Refrigerate for up to 3 days.

Nutrition:

Calories: 137

Fat: 11g

Protein: 2g

Carbs: 10g

Butternut Squash Mash

Preparation time: 15 minutes
Cooking time: 45 minutes
Servings: 4
Ingredients:

- Nonstick cooking spray
- 1 whole butternut squash, halved lengthwise, seeds and pulp removed
- 1 tablespoon olive oil
- Salt
- Freshly ground black pepper
- 3 or 4 garlic cloves, peeled
- 1 bunch fresh parsley, chopped
- ½ cup grated Parmesan cheese

Directions:

1. Preheat the oven to 375°F. Prepare a baking sheet lined with your aluminum foil and coat it with cooking spray.
2. Put the squash halves on the prepared baking sheet, cut-side up. Sprinkle with olive oil, season with salt and pepper, and place the garlic cloves and parsley into the cavities.
3. Bake within 45 minutes, until the squash can be pierced easily with a knife. Let cool until it can be handled safely.

4. Scoop the squash into a blender, along with the roasted garlic and parsley. Add the Parmesan cheese. Pulse for about 1 minute, until smooth.
5. Let cool before evenly dividing the squash among 4 single-serving 24-ounce meal prep containers. Refrigerate for up to 3 days.

Nutrition:

Calories: 176

Fat: 7g

Protein: 7g

Carbs: 25g

Balsamic Brussels Sprouts

Preparation time: 15 minutes

Cooking time: 40 minutes

Servings: 4

Ingredients:

- Nonstick cooking spray
- 1¼ pounds Brussels sprouts, trimmed and halved
- 2 tablespoons olive oil
- 1 teaspoon salt
- 1 teaspoon freshly ground black pepper
- ¼ cup balsamic glaze or reduction

Directions:

1. Preheat the oven to 400°F. Line a baking sheet with your aluminum foil and coat it with cooking spray.
2. On your prepared baking sheet, toss the Brussels sprouts, olive oil, salt, and pepper until evenly coated. Spread them into a single layer.
3. Bake within 18 minutes, or until the tops of some of the sprouts are lightly browned. Remove the baking sheet and coat the sprouts with the balsamic glaze.
4. Return to the oven and bake within 10 to 15 minutes more until the Brussels sprouts are browned. Let cool before evenly dividing the

sprouts among 4 single-serving 24-ounce meal prep containers. Refrigerate for up to 5 days.

Nutrition:

Calories: 141

Fat: 8g

Protein: 6g

Carbs: 20g

Roasted Cauliflower and Broccoli

Preparation time: 15 minutes

Cooking time: 20 minutes

Servings: 3

Ingredients:

- 1 cup broccoli florets
- ¼ cup butter
- Salt and black pepper, to taste
- 1 cup cauliflower florets
- ½ cup Parmesan cheese, grated

Directions:

1. Warm oven to 360 degrees and greases a baking tray. Mix broccoli florets, cauliflower florets, butter, salt, and black pepper in a bowl.
2. Put the veggie mixture on the baking tray and top with Parmesan cheese. Bake for about 20 minutes and remove from the oven to serve hot.

Nutrition:

Calories: 215

Carbs: 4.5g

Fats: 19.5g

Proteins: 7.7g

Mushroom Bacon Skewers

Preparation time: 15 minutes

Cooking time: 15 minutes

Servings: 4

Ingredients:

- 1-pound mushrooms
- 6 bacon strips
- 2 cups cheddar cheese, shredded
- Skewers
- 2 tablespoons mesquite seasoning

Directions:

1. Preheat the oven to 395 degrees and grease a baking tray. Season the mushrooms with mesquite seasoning.
2. Pierce one end of the bacon strip in the skewer, followed by the mushroom. Spear the other end of the bacon strip above the mushroom on the skewer.
3. Put the skewers on the baking tray and top with cheddar cheese. Bake for about 15 minutes and remove from oven to serve.

Nutrition:

Calories: 409

Carbs: 5.6g

Fats: 32.7g

Proteins: 23.9g

Creamed Peas

Preparation time: 15 minutes

Cooking time: 0 minutes

Servings: 3

Ingredients:

- 1 cup of water
- 1 cup fresh green peas
- 3 tablespoons butter
- Salt, to taste
- 1 cup heavy cream

Directions:

1. Heat the butter in the skillet and add fresh peas. Sauté for about 3 minutes and add salt, water, and heavy cream. Cook within 5 minutes on medium-low heat and dish out to serve hot.

Nutrition:

Calories: 279

Carbs: 8.1g

Fats: 26.5g

Proteins: 3.6g

Spinach Balls

Preparation time: 15 minutes
Cooking time: 30 minutes
Servings: 6
Ingredients:

- 1 cup cheddar cheese, grated
- 6 cup fresh spinach leaves, trimmed
- ½ cup butter
- ½ teaspoon garlic salt
- ¼ cup fresh parsley, finely chopped

Directions:

1. Warm oven to 400 degrees F and lightly greases a baking tray. Put the butter, garlic salt, cheddar cheese, fresh spinach leaves, and fresh parsley in a skillet.
2. Cook within 20 minutes on medium-low heat and dish out. Mold the spinach mixture into small-sized balls and arrange on the baking tray.
3. Transfer to the oven and bake within 10 minutes. Dish out and serve warm.

Nutrition:
Calories: 220
Carbs: 1.7g
Fats: 21.7g
Proteins: 5.8g

Cheesy Cauliflowers

Preparation time: 15 minutes

Cooking time: 20 minutes

Servings: 4

Ingredients:

- ¾ cup sour cream
- 1-pound cauliflower florets
- ¾ cup cheddar cheese, grated
- Salt and black pepper, to taste
- 3 tablespoons butter

Directions:

1. Warm oven to 400 degrees and lightly greases a baking dish. Put the sour cream, cauliflower, salt, and black pepper in a food processor.
2. Process until coarse and transfer to the baking dish. Top with cheddar cheese and melted butter. Bake for about 20 minutes and remove from oven to serve.

Nutrition:

Calories: 282

Carbs: 8.2g

Fats: 24.8g

Proteins: 9g

Tofu with Mushrooms

Preparation time: 15 minutes
Cooking time: 0 minutes
Servings: 6
Ingredients:

- 2 cups fresh mushrooms, chopped finely
- 8 tablespoons Parmesan cheese, shredded
- 2 blocks tofu, pressed and cubed into 1-inch pieces
- 8 tablespoons butter
- Salt
- ground black pepper, to taste

Directions:

1. Mix tofu, salt, and black pepper in a bowl. Put butter and seasoned tofu in a pan over medium-low heat.
2. Cook for about 5 minutes and stir in the mushrooms and Parmesan cheese. Cook for about 4 minutes, occasionally stirring, and dish onto a serving plate.

Nutrition:
Calories: 211
Carbs: 2g
Fats: 18.5g
Proteins: 11.5g

CPSIA information can be obtained
at www.ICGtesting.com
Printed in the USA
BVHW092049190421
605311BV00002B/176